Gemini

Also by Sally Kirkman

Aries
Taurus
Cancer
Leo
Virgo
Libra
Scorpio
Sagittarius
Capricorn
Aquarius
Pisces

SALLY KIRKMAN

Gemini

The Art of Living Well and Finding
Happiness According to Your Star Sign

HODDER

First published in Great Britain in 2018 by Hodder & Stoughton
An Hachette UK company

6

A CIP catalogue record for this title is available from the British Library

Hardback ISBN 978 1 473 67671 8

Typeset in Celeste 11.5/17 pt by Palimpsest Book Production Limited,
Falkirk, Stirlingshire

Printed and bound in Great Britain by Clays Ltd, Elcograf S.p.A.

Hodder & Stoughton policy is to use papers that are natural,
renewable and recyclable products and made from wood grown in
sustainable forests. The logging and manufacturing processes are expected
to conform to the environmental regulations of the country of origin.

Hodder & Stoughton Ltd
Carmelite House
50 Victoria Embankment
London EC4Y 0DZ

www.hodder.co.uk

Contents

· · · · ·

Introduction

· · · · ·

Before computers, books or a shared language, people were fascinated by the movement of the stars and planets. They created stories and myths around them. We know that the Babylonians were one of the first people to record the zodiac, a few hundred years BC.

In ancient times, people experienced a close connection to the earth and the celestial realm. The adage 'As above, so below', that the movement of the planets and stars mirrored life on earth and human affairs, made perfect sense. Essentially, we were all one, and ancient people sought symbolic meaning in everything around them.

We are living in a very different world now, in

which scientific truth is paramount; yet many people are still seeking meaning. In a world where you have an abundance of choice, dominated by the social media culture that allows complete visibility into other people's lives, it can be hard to feel you belong or find purpose or think that the choices you are making are the right ones.

It's this calling for something more, the sense that there's a more profound truth beyond the objective and scientific, that leads people to astrology and similar disciplines that embrace a universal truth, an intuitive knowingness. Today astrology has a lot in common with spirituality, meditation, the Law of Attraction, a desire to know the cosmic order of things.

Astrology means 'language of the stars' and people today are rediscovering the usefulness of ancient wisdom. The universe is always talking to you; there are signs if you listen and the more you tune in, the more you feel guided by life. This is one of astrology's significant benefits, helping you to make sense of an increasingly unpredictable world.

Used well, astrology can guide you in making the best possible decisions in your life. It's an essential skill in your personal toolbox that enables you to navigate the ups and downs of life consciously and efficiently.

About this book

Astrology is an ancient art that helps you find meaning in the world. The majority of people to this day know their star sign, and horoscopes are growing increasingly popular in the media and online.

The modern reader understands that star signs are a helpful reference point in life. They not only offer valuable self-insight and guidance, but are indispensable when it comes to understanding other people, and living and working together in harmony.

This new and innovative pocket guide updates the ancient tradition of astrology to make it relevant and topical for today. It distils the wisdom of the star signs into an up-to-date format that's easy to read and digest, and fun and informative too. Covering a broad range of topics, it offers you insight and understanding into many different areas of your life. There are some unique sections you won't find anywhere else.

The style of the guide is geared towards you being able to maximise your strengths, so you can live well and use your knowledge of your star sign to your advantage. The more in tune you are with your zodiac sign, the higher your potential to lead a happy and fulfilled life.

The guide starts with a quick introduction to your star sign, in bullet point format. This not only reveals your star sign's ancient ruling principles, but brings astrology up-to-date, with your star sign mission, an appropriate quote for your sign and how best to describe your star sign in a tweet.

The first chapter is called 'Be True To Your Sign' and is one of the most important sections in the guide. It's a comprehensive look at all aspects of your star sign, helping define what makes you special, and explaining how the rich symbolism of your zodiac sign can reveal more about your character. For example, being born at a specific time of year and in a particular season is significant in itself.

This chapter focuses in depth on the individual attributes of your star sign in a way that's positive and uplifting. It offers a holistic view of your sign and is meant to inspire you. Within this section, you find out the reasons why your star sign traits and characteristics are unique to you.

There's a separate chapter towards the end of the guide that takes this star sign information to a new level. It's called 'Your Cosmic Gifts and Talents' and tells you what's individual about you from your star sign perspective. Most importantly, it highlights your skills and strengths, offering you clear examples of how to make the most of your natural birthright.

The guide touches on another important aspect of your star sign, in the chapters entitled 'Your Shadow Side' and 'Your Star Sign Secrets'. This reveals the potential weaknesses inherent within your star sign, and the tricks and habits you can fall into if you're not aware of them. The star sign secrets might surprise you.

There's guidance here about what you can focus on to minimise the shadow side of your star sign, and this is linked in particular to your opposite sign of the zodiac. You learn how opposing forces complement each other when you hold both ends of the spectrum, enabling them to work together.

Essentially, the art of astrology is about how to find balance in your life, to gain a sense of universal or cosmic order, so you feel in flow rather than pulled in different directions.

Other chapters in the guide provide revealing information about your love life and sex life. There are cosmic tips on how to work to your star sign strengths so you can attract and keep a fulfilling relationship, and lead a joyful sex life. There's also a guide to your love compatibility with all twelve star signs.

Career, money and prosperity is another essential section in the guide. These chapters offer you vital information on your purpose in life, and how to make the most of your potential out in the world. Your star sign skills and strengths are revealed, including what sort of job or profession suits you.

There are also helpful suggestions about what to avoid and what's not a good choice for you. There's a list of traditional careers associated with your star sign, to give you ideas about where you can excel in life if you require guidance on your future direction.

Also, there are chapters in the book on practical matters, like your health and well-being, your food and diet. These recommend the right kind of exercise for you, and how you can increase your vitality and nurture your mind, body and soul, depending on your star sign. There are individual yoga poses and tarot cards that have been carefully selected for you.

Further chapters reveal unique star sign information about your image and style. This includes whether there's a particular fashion that suits you, and how you can accentuate your look and make the most of your body.

There are even chapters that can help you decide where to go on holiday and who with, and how to decorate your home. There are some fun sections, including ideal gifts for your star sign, and ideas for films, books and music specific to your star sign.

Also, the guide has a comprehensive birthday section so you can find out which famous people share your birthday. You can discover who else is born under your star sign, people who may be your role models and whose careers or gifts you can aspire to. There are celebrity examples throughout the guide too, revealing more about the unique characteristics of your star sign.

At the end of the guide, there's a Question and Answer section, which explains the astrological terms used in the guide. It also offers answers to some general questions that often arise around astrology.

This theme is continued in a useful section entitled Additional Information. This describes the symmetry of astrology and shows you how different patterns connect the twelve star signs. If you're a beginner to astrology, this is your next stage, learning about the elements, the modes and the houses.

View this book as your blueprint, your guide to you and your future destiny. Enjoy discovering astrological revelations about you, and use this pocket guide to learn how to live well and find happiness according to your star sign.

A QUICK GUIDE TO GEMINI

• • • • •

Gemini Birthdays: 21 May to 20 June

Zodiac Symbol: The Twins

Ruling Planet: Mercury

Mode/Element: Mutable Air

Colour: Yellow, multicoloured

Part of the Body: Hands, arms, shoulders and lungs

Day of the Week: Wednesday

Top Traits: Quick-thinking, Agile, Youthful

Your Star Sign Mission: to use language to transcend boundaries, to hold contradictory beliefs without having to resolve them

Best At: multitasking, talking, flexibility, curiosity, thinking on your feet, playing practical jokes, being a jack of all trades, doubling up, all forms of communication

Weaknesses: stretching the truth, deceiving, being flippant or fake, easily bored, superficial

Key Phrase: I communicate

Gemini Quote: 'Be careful of the words you say, keep them short and sweet. You never know, from day to day, which ones you'll have to eat'. Anonymous

How to describe Gemini in a Tweet: Young-spirited, a butterfly. Talks for England, loves chatter & gossip. Always on the move. Has two of everything; names, phones

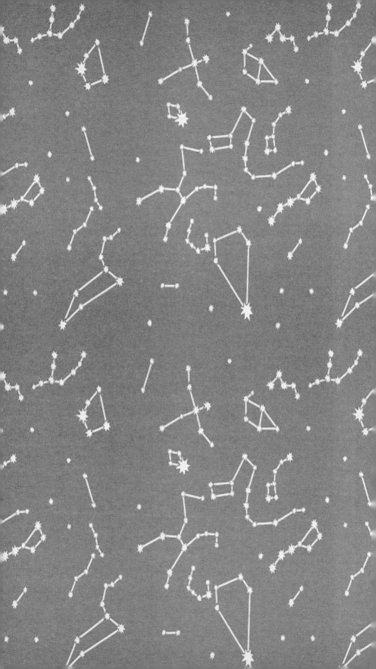

Be True To Your Sign

• • • • •

You are the communicator of the zodiac with a quick mind and a lively wit. Always on the go, the archetypal Gemini is curious, alert, funny, vivacious and adheres firmly to the motto that 'variety is the spice of life'.

You are the third sign of the zodiac, the last month of spring in the northern hemisphere. You are springlike in your approach to life, full of bounce and verve, with a colourful and sunny personality. Gemini is definitely one of the extrovert signs.

You don't always have time to stop and smell the roses, however, as you're usually too busy with a long list of things to do and people to talk to. Gemini is one of the mutable signs, whose common traits are versatility and adaptability, and all the mutable signs are of a dual nature. Your zodiac symbol is the twins, representing the power of two in the Gemini psyche.

You take this one stage further because you're not only adept at doing two things at once, but you're an excellent multitasker too. Multiplicity is a crucial component of the Gemini type; your character is multifaceted, and Gemini rules all things multicoloured. You are the archetypal jack of all trades, the wheeler-dealer of the zodiac, and you have the gift of the gab to match.

There are specific reasons for this. Firstly, Gemini is one of the air signs, and air is the element that represents networking, social connections, thinking, talking and the sharing of ideas.

Secondly, Gemini rules the third house in the astrology wheel, symbolising communication and the domain of language and the mind. Put the two together, and you are masterful at the written and spoken word and a natural linguist. You are the zodiac's reporter, journalist, storyteller, presenter and a lively raconteur.

If you're a typical Gemini, you're a motormouth whose thought processes fire on all cylinders, and you love nothing more than a gossip, chat and catch-up. Even without someone to talk to, you won't stop talking but will chat to your pets, your plants, your car . . . anyone or anything who'll stay in one place.

Silence and quiet aren't Gemini's natural habitat; instead, you prefer to have the noise of the radio in the background or be in the midst of activity, immersed in the hustle and bustle of life. Wherever people gather, and there's something new to see and learn, this is where you feel most at home.

You talk with your hands, and Gemini rules the hands and arms in astrology. In fact, the classic Gemini rarely sits still or stands still for long. You were born to move.

The third house rules transport, short trips and commuting and if you're typical of your star sign, you will love being in taxis and on buses and trains. There's always the possibility of meeting someone new as you happily watch the world go by. You take people-watching to a whole new level and, if you're true to your sign, you find other people fascinating.

This makes sense when you learn about your ruling planet Mercury and its mythological associations. Mercury was the winged messenger who would communicate and run errands between the gods. Speedy, youthful and fleet-footed with wings on his heels, Mercury was comfortable with mortals and immortals alike. No wonder that, as a Gemini, you're renowned for being a gregarious extrovert and nippy and fast on your feet.

It's your mind, however, where you excel, and you are one of life's eternal students. You're always ready to learn, about anything you're remotely interested in – and as a Gemini, you're interested in most things. Your mind rarely switches off, and you are the trivia king/queen of the zodiac.

If you're a classic Gemini, you have an incredible breadth of knowledge thanks to your insatiable curiosity. What you don't always find so easy, however, is to complete what you start because you're quickly bored and you often try to do more than one thing at once. Five books on the go at the same time? That's a Gemini trait.

You have quick reflexes too, and you can change your ideas and perspective frequently. The fact that Gemini is a mutable (changeable) air (thought processes) sign means you have to teach your mind to sit still. You're an expert at making snap decisions but not so skilled at standing firm in your convictions, and this can lead to you feeling ambivalent or uncertain.

It is your lively nature, however, that helps to keep you youthful. Plus, the fact that you are both physically and mentally active. You have a young spirit and your playful attitude, and livewire frame of mind, mean that you tend to age well. In fact, one of Gemini's names is the Peter Pan of the zodiac.

This is also linked to the mythology behind your sign, and the story of Gemini's star constellation. The two brightest stars were named after twin brothers, Castor and Pollux, one mortal, one immortal.

When the mortal brother, Castor, was killed in battle, Pollux appealed to the gods to be able to share his immortality, which was agreed. The brothers subsequently alternated between heaven and earth and remained 'forever young'. The quest for divine immortality i.e. how to stay young can play a significant part in your Gemini journey.

This Gemini tale flags up the theme of duality and one of your roles in life is learning how to hold contradictory thoughts and beliefs. Add to this your love of word games, your skill and ability with language and a mischievous impulse to play devil's advocate, and you win more arguments and debates than anyone. You are the monkey of the zodiac, cheeky and impish and often a lover of practical jokes.

Even when you're butting heads with someone or engaged in a war of words, you prefer to keep things light. The classic Gemini rarely takes life or self too seriously.

Mostly, you're the zodiac's social butterfly, always wanting to learn more and know more about life, people and facts. If you can have a laugh and a joke along the way and bring joy and lightness into other people's lives, your role as a Gemini is complete.

Your Shadow Side

It is said about your star sign that you have a split personality. This is rarely true, but what you do have is an incredibly lively mind that flits back and forth and is continuously on the go.

In fact, your mind can be so lively that you often speak without thinking. Your mercurial nature means you forget what you said and change your version of things repeatedly. In the midst of the confusion, you create your own truth and perceive the world in your own unique way.

You're a good storyteller too, and this can get turned on its head. Sometimes, you might be accused of 'telling stories', and you are known for your ability to embellish the truth. This may be done purely innocently, but there is a cunning and sneaky shadow side to your Gemini character.

When you fall deep into your mind and end up speaking your thoughts with no filter attached, you can gain a reputation for being controversial or two-faced. This is the shadow side of your Gemini nature that loves to cause trouble, to be provocative and duplicitous.

The problem comes when you allow your mind to dominate and you lose touch with your emotions and compassion. Then you have the potential for being a cynic. Gemini's shadow at its most extreme is the troll or liar.

In mythology, your ruler Mercury was a trickster and a thief, and so he was put to work as a messenger of the gods to keep him out of trouble. If you allow your shadow side to take hold, you too can fall victim to the Gemini stereotype of the dark twin and turn mischief into mayhem.

All star signs can learn from their opposite sign in the zodiac and, for you, this is Sagittarius. Sagittarius represents truth and justice and takes the broader perspective. Ruled by Jupiter, the protective planet, Sagittarius can teach your sign of Gemini to rise above petty squabbles and to be inclusive rather than divisive. It can help you reorient your moral compass, so you use your words and actions for noble purposes rather than as weapons to attack and deceive.

There is another level to your shadow side that is connected to the part of your nature that is brooding and irrational. You often keep your dark twin hidden away, not wanting to show this side of your personality to anyone, or sometimes even admit it to yourself. You are two-faced insomuch as you are capable of putting on a happy face when inside you're crying.

Note that in mythology, your ruler Mercury didn't just run around on happy errands all day long. In fact, it was Mercury who guided souls to the entrance of the Underworld, and he had one foot in the world of darkness and the dead, where sorrow resides.

Sometimes, you need to allow yourself to unravel, to go to darker places, to be silent, because it's only by so doing that you discover hidden riches; and when you emerge back into the light, you're wiser and stronger for your experience. This brings new depths to your flighty butterfly spirit.

Your Star Sign Secrets

Shhh, don't tell anyone but your greatest fear is that, when it comes to navigating your own life, you will make the wrong decisions. Your lively mind is so attuned to infinite possibilities that you talk yourself in and out of different situations and tie yourself in knots. It can become exhausting as you try to work out the best thing to do. In fact, sometimes you find it easier to do nothing and put off the big decisions, because that way at least you won't make the wrong choice! This is Gemini's star sign secret.

You have another secret too, which is related to your shadow side. You would prefer to tell a white lie than deal with an uncomfortable situation or get embroiled in an emotional exchange. The problem occurs when you're caught out, which lands you in more trouble. This can swiftly escalate into a spectacular case of mental gymnastics as you try to talk your way out of your predicament.

Your Love Life

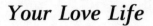

Knowing about your star sign is an absolute essential when it comes to love and relationships. Once you understand what drives you, nurtures you and keeps you happy in love, then you can be true to who you are rather than try to be someone you're not.

Plus, once you recognise your weak points when it comes to relationships (and everyone has them), you can learn to moderate them and focus instead on boosting your strengths to find happiness in love.

> **KEY CONCEPTS:** two marriages, an unconventional love life, go where love leads, self-love, people person

Cosmic Tip: You can't work out love in your brain: feel it with all of your body and soul first, then engage your mind.

When it comes to the Gemini love life, this is where the whimsical, mercurial side of your nature is often most evident. You are a changeable character, and this doesn't always stem from your emotions or your heart but instead from your thought processes.

You can talk yourself in and out of a relationship faster than anyone. One minute you think a new partner is fantastic, and the next minute you've changed your mind and decided you're completely incompatible. Or you meet someone new who wins you over with their charm, wit and intelligence, and your attention is instantly hooked onto them.

Not only can this be confusing for the other person or people involved, but being so indecisive and changeable also makes your own life incredibly complicated, and you end up with a reputation for being fickle and flighty.

This is why it's so important to know yourself and, in particular, what works for you as a Gemini when it comes to love.

Indeed, you won't last long with a partner if they don't have an intellect and wit to match your own. This is how you connect with other people, and it's why making friends and meeting new people is a cinch for the typical Gemini.

You are usually natural in social situations and your love of life, added to your fascination for the human race, means you are rarely lonely. In fact, if you're a typical Gemini, you're probably a favourite member of a whole host of different groups.

Also, it helps to work out what you want from a relationship and why you want to be with someone. At some level, it does have to be a mind decision for you, because that's how you process everything.

That's not to say you won't be bowled over by love at some point in your life and meet a twin flame, very possibly more than once. When your heart opens, you leap in and follow where it leads. This can be both exciting and scary for the Gemini individual, as a love that's heartfelt is by its definition irrational. Sometimes, you feel safer basking in the recesses of your mind rather than venturing into heart and soul territory.

Remember the dual theme of Gemini too. It is rare for you lovely Gemini individuals to meet someone early in your life and for that person to be your partner at the end of your life. The classic Gemini stereotype is that you will marry twice or fall in love fully and deeply twice in your life.

Now that's not to say it won't work being with one partner for the majority of your adult life. If it is going to last, then you need a partner who understands your mercurial nature and is just as keen as you are for a life filled with fun, variety and stimulation.

Line up new adventures together, live abroad for a while, mingle in engaging social and professional circles, share your interests and be proactive in love. Most importantly, give one another free rein to explore and experiment, and that might mean sexually. Talk through all your options and if it works for both of you, great.

Some Gemini marriages work better when you take time away from each other, and you're not tied at the hip. Take Helena Bonham Carter (26 May), for example, who lived in the house next door to her husband and father of her two children, Tim Burton.

There is a side of your Gemini nature that doesn't fit comfortably into a conventional or traditional role, so spread your Gemini butterfly wings and embrace who you are. Be honest too, if there's a side of your nature that fears commitment, and you know that heart-opening, loving relationships can fuel your insecurities.

The truth is you are one of the most interesting, witty, stimulating and lively of all the star signs, so finding one person in your life to keep you entertained for years is a big ask. In a relationship, don't rely on your partner to be everything to you, but encourage them to lead an independent life and do the same yourself.

There are other options available too, for your playful sign of Gemini. If you want an exciting love life with numerous partners along the way, be accepting of yourself and lead the life that you choose. Team up with other people who have a similar attitude to love and relationships.

Also, you age well, and it's not unusual for you to want a younger lover and partner as you get older. The classic example is Joan Collins (23 May), who married her fifth husband, Percy Gibson, in her late 60s. There's a twenty-two-year age gap between them, Joan Collins being the elder.

It's important to ask yourself whether you think that the fairytale 'happy-ever-after' relationship is a possibility, or it's not part of your Gemini story. For example, if you're living a typical Gemini lifestyle, surrounded by a diverse group of friends with many interests, hobbies and activities to fill your days, you might not have time for love. You could be happier and less bored enjoying a more varied lifestyle.

You're a people person at heart and rather than lead a 'normal life', why not invent a new normal and do what you do best: live in the moment.

Your Love Matches

Some star signs are a better love match for you than others. The classic combinations are the other two star signs from the same element as your sign, air; in Gemini's case, Libra and Aquarius.

All the air signs match your lust for life but you can out-talk anyone. In fact, your friendly and bubbly personality is your greatest asset in the game of love. You can be extremely persuasive, with top-notch wooing skills that sweep other people off their feet. Whoever you choose to impress, you have first-class credentials to make an impact and attract attention.

It's also important to recognise that any star sign match can be a good match if you're willing to learn from each other and use astrological insight to understand more about what makes the other person tick. Here's a quick guide to your love matches with all twelve star signs:

Gemini–Aries: Sexy Sextiles

There's always something to talk about or do in this relationship, although tempers can flare if hot air overheats. Turn arguments into humorous anecdotes and you two have a rapport like a house on fire. Laugh-out-loud moments and witty repartee go hand in hand.

Gemini–Taurus: Next-Door Neighbours

Gemini is flighty and restless, while Taurus loves comfort and routine. Together you enjoy a giggle, but you have to be prepared to meet the other halfway. You keep Taurus entertained, and Taurus teaches you that consistency brings rewards.

Gemini–Gemini: Two Peas In A Pod

A youthful match, you two are on a permanent speed date. With bags of energy, you are like brother and sister one moment and starry-eyed lovers the next. Trust may be an issue as you both love to flirt, but if you can hold each other's attention, this is a lively and fun combination.

Gemini–Cancer: Next-Door Neighbours

You tend to run a mile from strong emotions whereas Cancer needs a partner who understands them on an emotional level. If you can transform Cancer's mood swings and keep things light, while

Cancer nurtures the childlike side of your nature, this pairing can thrive.

Gemini–Leo: Sexy Sextiles

Life needs to be fun for you two, and this match thrives when you put play before work. Both of you love to be centre of attention in your own way: you are the storyteller, while Leo is the drama king or queen. The $100 question is whether you can offer Leo the attention s/he craves.

Gemini–Virgo: Squaring Up To Each Other

You are both lovers of all things chatty, the written word and versatility. Together you are fun, witty and slightly eccentric. If it starts to feel like you're best mates rather than lovers, turn to a self-help manual on loving relations or spice up your sex life to keep romance alive.

Gemini–Libra: In Your Element

If you two have nothing to talk about, there's something wrong. This is one of the chattiest combinations in the zodiac, as you are both naturally sociable. You like to flit through life whereas Libra loves to be in love, and trust will play a big part in the success of this relationship.

Gemini–Scorpio: Soulmates

Gemini and Scorpio is a common combination as you both have a thirst for knowledge and love to find things out. Life is a mystery to be explored to the full. Sometimes you need a break from each other, however, as Scorpio is deep and intense whereas you are chatty and light.

Gemini–Sagittarius: Opposites Attract

Gemini is always on the move, flighty, witty and loves gossip. Sagittarius is the traveller, a seeker of truth and meaning in life. Together you can have lots of fun and learn from each other. A youthful duo with a mutual love of life.

Gemini–Capricorn: Soulmates

Gemini and Capricorn may not seem to have much in common, but Capricorn's dry and offbeat humour resonates with your witty nature. Your thirst for knowledge and Capricorn's wisdom and experience sit well with each other as long as boredom isn't a problem.

Gemini–Aquarius: In Your Element

You two have a lot in common, but it takes something special to move your friendship on to the next stage. You're both keen on doing things differently and ringing the changes. An open relationship is a strong possibility, and a wide circle of friends is a given.

Gemini–Pisces: Squaring Up To Each Other

This is a cosmic coupling, and you two are a fun duo who love finding things out, exploring new ideas and venturing into magical and mystical realms together. At its best, you are crazy and romantic buddies who walk hand in hand through life together.

Your Sex Life

• • • • •

If variety is the spice of Gemini's life, then your sex life must be spicy indeed. Sex is an opportunity for you to try things out, see what you like and what you don't and explore the physical body to the full.

Sometimes the classic Gemini can take it or leave it when it comes to sex, and for sex to be gratifying, it must not only be fun but also be something you can process through your mind. Sex without talking can be a no-no for you, as it's often the words and everything related to the words that turns you on the most.

If you're a typical Gemini, you will love the art of flirting. This is an opportunity to use your smart wit to the full, to seduce another person with the art of language. Sexy banter, sexting, sharing provocative messages with your lover; this is what turns you on.

Similarly, you can be immensely stimulated by reading about sex, talking about sex or writing down your sexual experiences. The phrase 'sex is all in the mind' applies to your sign of Gemini entirely.

Being articulate can be an asset when it comes to sexual pleasure because you're more likely to ask for what you want and communicate well with your lover. Use your Gemini skills to maximise the physical experience.

Being a lover of variety means that you can become bored if sex is the same every time you participate. If you're in a long-term relationship, it's vital to spice things up in your sex life. Otherwise, you'll lose interest or look elsewhere.

If it's fun, do it, whether you like dressing up, roleplay, experimenting with sex toys, reading erotic literature or any other sex-extra activity that stimulates you both. You need new fantasies, new sexual positions and maybe even new lovers to hold your interest. If you're coupled up, swinging parties are one way to keep your sex life full of surprises.

The theme of duality tends to play out in the Gemini sex life. For example, you might go through a phase where you have more than one lover on the go and, at some point in your life, you will likely end up in a triangle love situation. Take this theme one step further, and a favourite Gemini sexual fantasy is a threesome with two people to pleasure you at one time.

You are one of the most broad-minded of all the star signs, and you find all kinds of people fascinating, which is why some Gemini individuals are bisexual and willing to experiment.

You are often a strong advocate of the LGBT community, whatever your sexual orientation. One of the most famous transgender celebrities of recent times is Laverne Cox (29 May). Rising to prominence on the TV show *Orange Is The New Black*, Laverne is the first transgender person to be nominated for an Emmy and appear on the cover of *Time* magazine.

The initials Q – queer or questioning – and I – intersex – are commonly added to the LGBT acronym. In mythology, Hermaphroditus was the son of Hermes, another name for your ruler Mercury, and the goddess Aphrodite. Anything goes for your multifaceted and extraordinary sign of Gemini when it comes to sex. Theoretically, if you can think of it, you can do it.

GEMINI ON A FIRST DATE

- you like to keep your date guessing

- you turn up with two of something – bags, phones, personalities

- you meet in a buzzing and lively venue

- you do most of the talking

- you can't make up your mind what next

Your Friends and Family

As a Gemini, you are one of the best friends going because you've always got something to talk about. You are the zodiac's chief gossip, holder of trivial information, and you have a mind that continually whizzes in and out of different parts of your brain, re-emerging with new snippets.

Plus, it's not all about me, me, me when you're a Gemini. You are genuinely interested and fascinated by other people. It doesn't matter where you are either; if there's someone to talk to, you'll be the first to open up the conversation.

You love finding out facts too, and you rarely waste a minute of your time. If you're in the car or on the bus, you'll listen to an audiobook rather than sit silently. Another reason why you always have lots to talk about; you're continually curious and learning about life.

Another reason why you're a brilliant friend is your sense of humour. You love playing with words, which includes telling stories and jokes and using your mental agility to mimic other people. You're naturally funny, and you like puns, word games and double entendres. You have a mischievous sense of humour and you love practical jokes too.

You're not the best person to turn to, however, if someone wants to moan or complain or they're dragging heavy emotional baggage behind them. Ideally, you prefer to keep relations light. You'll do your best to cheer a friend up, but you won't have much patience with anyone who stays down in the dumps.

If you're a typical Gemini, you often get involved with neighbours and your local community, and in astrology, both sets of people are linked to Gemini's sector of the astrology wheel, the third house.

This isn't surprising considering you'll talk to anyone. The people you're most likely to meet when you're out and about are the ones who live close by. Having a stable community of local people in your life is both comforting and entertaining. This is where you feel you belong. Having friends to call on and activities to get involved in close to home suits your sociable personality.

You often end up as spokesperson for your neighbourhood, whether you're campaigning for a local cause or bringing people together. This is where you excel as you can combine your Gemini social butterfly nature with your straight talking.

Siblings belong to the third house, and your relationship with your brothers, sisters or cousins often plays a significant role in your life. There might be a particular story to tell or perhaps a close bond – or the opposite, a feud.

One classic example is Noel Gallagher (29 May) and his brother Liam, ex-band members in Oasis, who famously share a turbulent relationship.

As long as you don't have any family feuds, you tend to enjoy meeting up with your relatives. The bigger the get-together, the better, and you usually prefer a social occasion where you come together, have fun and then you all return to your own lives. If family connections feel heavy or relatives drag you down, you won't want to spend too much time in their company.

Your lively nature requires careful handling, and it helps to find a healthy balance between socialising and enjoying downtime. If you think of the Gemini mind as a computer, it needs time to reset and power back up before you can use it fully again.

An overdose of emotional friends, too much partying, work relations at warp speed and you're more than ready to go home, put on your PJs and binge-watch your favourite programmes.

When it comes to intimate relationships, and especially the decision whether to parent or not, there are an infinite number of possibilities. 'One size fits all' does not do justice to your individual nature. Whether you remain single and become the best aunt or uncle, godparent or life parent, you do family in your unique style.

With Gemini's theme of duality, the ideal number of children would be two. Your sign encompasses multiplicity, however, so don't discount adoption or some pets if having children is not an option for you.

Josephine Baker (3 June) was a fascinating character in true Gemini style. She was an entertainer and French Resistance agent in the Second World War who married four times but also had affairs with women. When Josephine couldn't have children herself, she adopted her 'Rainbow Tribe', ten boys and two girls from different nationalities, defying convention to create her own family.

A modern example is Angelina Jolie (4 June), actor and humanitarian, also known for her 'rainbow children', three adopted and three biological. The multifaceted nature of Gemini can be expressed on many different levels.

Your Health and Well-Being

> **KEY CONCEPTS:** count your steps, make fitness fun, calming herbs and relaxation techniques, healthy snacks, a balanced diet

When you're a lively air sign with a mind that's always on the go, it's vital you find a way to burn off your excess energy. Admittedly, it helps that it's not only your mind that's quick; if you're a typical Gemini, you're a fast mover too.

In fact, even if you don't want to do any traditional exercise, you can quite happily incorporate extra movement into your daily life. For example, run up and down stairs instead of getting the escalator, or skip the tube or bus journey and walk instead. It's an excellent idea for you to count your steps with an activity tracker. You might be surprised how far you walk in a day.

The key to exercising for the typical Gemini is to forget the words 'regular and routine' and replace them with 'variety and fun'. Whenever anything becomes a chore in your daily schedule, or you start to get bored with your routine, this is when you can start to talk yourself out of going to the gym or attending your weekly sport or exercise class.

Instead, chop and change your exercise routine and do whatever takes your fancy, whenever it suits you. If you're a typical Gemini, you won't have a regular or routine lifestyle anyway, as you prefer to be spontaneous and ring the changes.

If you are an archetypal Gemini, you're light on your feet and good with your hands, so play to your strengths when it comes to keeping fit. You might enjoy dancing, football, aerobics or athletics, all ideal sports for your sprightly nature. Tennis, squash and table tennis require dexterity and fast reactions, both Gemini traits, so get those hands moving.

Gemini rules the hands, arms and shoulders and also the lungs. Note that there are two of each, fitting for Gemini's theme of duality. Keep your arms strong by doing weights or daily plank exercises and boost your vitality to benefit your lungs.

Nervous tension can be a Gemini issue, and you can go through a smoking phase in your adult life. A better strategy is to learn to breathe correctly and to slow your breathing through regular relaxation exercises. This will help your focus too.

If you're aware that you have a typical Gemini monkey mind, then any discipline that helps you to be mindful and meditative is worth pursuing. You often learn to slow down with age, but when you're younger, you rarely see the point.

If your mind is so overactive that you suffer from insomnia, use Chinese medicine, herbs or B vitamins to soothe your nerves. Valerian is associated with your ruling planet Mercury, as are chamomile and lavender, all known for their relaxing and soporific qualities.

It's also a good idea to limit your time on technological gadgets because you can quickly lose track of time when you're plugged into the internet. You might forget why you went on the internet or social media in the first place, as your Gemini mind races along at top speed and you are quickly diverted by interesting snippets of gossip and information. Build some quiet time into your busy schedule.

Gemini and Food

Aries is the first sign of the zodiac, and seeds and grows food, Taurus is the second sign, and cultivates and cooks food; Gemini is the third sign, and you enjoy nothing more than eating, writing and talking about food.

Gemini TV chefs are some of the best and, between them, they have sold millions of cookery books. Three well-known UK cookery writers are cheeky chappie Jamie Oliver (27 May), national treasure Delia Smith (18 June) and Ella Woodward (31 May), otherwise known as Deliciously Ella.

For a typical Gemini, eating food is something you often find difficult to do on its own. One of your favourite pastimes is eating out in a restaurant with an exciting group of people. You don't want music so loud that you can't hear the conversation, but you love the conviviality of sharing food and talking with friends.

Even at home, however, unless you're having a family meal, you might find it impossible to sit down at the table to eat with no phone, book or TV or radio programme to keep you occupied. Eating a meal in silence by yourself is a rare occasion for the classic Gemini. A good exercise for Gemini is to learn to savour your food slowly and to eat mindfully.

What usually happens is you want food that cooks quickly, and you eat standing up in the kitchen. Also, unless you have set mealtimes, you can soon resort to snacking or forget to eat altogether.

This doesn't aid your metabolism, and as you often run off nervous energy, it's important to try to establish a regular eating routine. What will help is to ensure you have healthy snacks to hand, such as nuts and dried fruit.

The ideal Gemini food is finger food, tasty morsels that give you a variety of flavours. Tapas and mezze platters are perfect for the Gemini diet. Ideally, try to include all food groups in a meal and keep the majority of what you eat healthy and light. It is easy for you to finish off a packet of biscuits, for example, just because you get distracted.

Foods ruled by your sign have strong, distinctive flavours and include fennel, aniseed and liquorice. Beans too are a Gemini food and an excellent source of protein as well as good for satisfying your hunger.

You're best when you stick to a moderate, balanced diet and allow yourself wine, beer or coffee, as long as you don't take it to the extreme. Make food and a healthy lifestyle fun by participating in both with good friends by your side.

Do You Look Like A Gemini?

You are the Peter Pan of the zodiac, and many Gemini individuals come in tiny packages. The typical Gemini figure is short or small, and even if you're taller, you're likely to be slender and willowy. You're agile and continuously on the go. In fact, you rarely stand still for long, which is why you tend not to put on weight quickly.

Look out for the graceful arms and hands that are always moving or gesticulating. You talk with your hands and can be quite nervous or fidgety and play with your hair, for example. Sometimes your quick movements are almost bird-like, and both your hands and feet are often diminutive or dainty.

There's often a cute smile ready to break out on your face, and your facial features tend to be small and delicate. Your expressive eyes are always mischievous, and they sparkle with life, darting here, there and everywhere, not missing a trick.

Your Style and Image

You are as fickle when it comes to fashion as you are in all areas of your life. Your sign is the chameleon of the zodiac, continually changing your ideas and, when it comes to your look, frequently changing your style.

You do like your fashion to be current, however, and you tend to have your finger on the pulse of what's in and what's out, what's popular and what's not. Even if you don't wear the latest trends, more likely than not you know what they are.

Take Danielle Bernstein (28 May), for example, who is a top fashion blogger for her brand 'We Wore What' based in New York. In 2017, she made the *Forbes 30 Under 30* Art & Style list, a classic example of an up-to-date Gemini trendspotter.

Gemini's style is rarely dull, and you are attracted to colourful, individual and fun clothes. The classic Gemini colour is yellow but you look good in multi-coloured garments, and you're someone who can get away with wearing checks and stripes. All your clothes must be comfortable to wear and easy to care for, and preferably light in colour. Trainers are your ideal footwear, so you can move around quickly.

Silver and sparkly clothes suit you and, as Gemini rules the arms and shoulders, show them off. For the Gemini woman, a halter-neck or a vest top work, if weather permits, and for a glamorous event an off-the-shoulder dress is bang on trend.

Lots of jewellery looks great on the classic Gemini, especially bracelets, bangles and rings, which accentuate your active hands. Anything that jingles fits your vivacious nature.

Regular manicures keep your hands and nails looking beautiful, which in turn makes you feel good. Also, your Gemini spirit loves tattoos, especially words or a fun, quirky symbol.

Your youthful spirit means you tend to look good in 'young' clothes, e.g. dungarees, a backpack, even hot pants. A classic example is Kylie Minogue (28 May), who famously wore tiny gold hot pants in the video for 'Spinning Around'.

Gemini men tend to be dapper with a metrosexual style and to care about their looks. One of Gemini's most significant fashion icons is singer-song-writer, Prince (7 June), who always demonstrated the ever-changing Gemini style.

Your Home

Your Ideal Gemini Home:

Your sign of Gemini wants two of everything, and that includes homes. A bijou residence in the middle of a bustling city where you can people-watch, and a light and airy luxury villa somewhere exotic, filled inside and out with flowers, colour and happy people.

As a typical Gemini, you love variety, and you like a busy home. You need space to move around, and you're more attracted to light, bright colour schemes than anything dark or heavy. A mix of styles, old and modern, often appeals to your magpie nature, and you collect objects and knick-knacks from different eras and stages of your life.

Just as an open-plan office suits you at work, your ideal home is also open-plan, perhaps with movable screens to divide up space. You have a love of novelty and a thirst for knowledge, and both will be evident in the place you live. A coffee table in the lounge will be full of books and magazines to grab your interest and teach you something new. Puzzle books and games appeal to your Gemini nature.

Gemini's colour is yellow, but other spring colours will brighten up your home and lift your spirits too, such as off-white, lavender and apple green. When it comes to soft furnishings, you could choose multicoloured styles, small geometric patterns, checks and mixes.

The combination is the key, and you rarely appreciate a home that's all one colour and perfectly coordinated, much preferring to see a variety of styles on display. For the same reason, you often like fancy wallpaper featuring writing or images of birds, butterflies or flowers.

Because you're easily bored, it is essential that you're able to change your surroundings as and when you want. Go for things in your home that aren't too expensive, so you can replace them, or swap furniture around when the fancy takes you.

You tend to like constant noise in your home too, especially if you live alone. You might have the radio turned on in the background or a pet, to keep things lively. The ideal Gemini companion is a parrot or mynah bird who'll talk to you or a budgerigar that's continuously chirruping.

Also, your home must be a shrine to communication, as it's imperative that you can make contact efficiently with other people and the outside world. At least two phones are the Gemini style.

Entertainment must be a priority too. Ideally, you'll have plenty of room for friends and family to sit in the lounge or garden, a kitchen where people can gather and a dining table big enough to accommodate a friendly crowd.

Make sure you have pinboards prominent in the hall, kitchen or office, where you can put up anecdotes, favourite quotes, cartoons and flyers for activities or classes close to home. You like to create a lively buzz in the place you live. Why not invest in an Italian-style espresso or coffee machine and create your very own cafe-style atmosphere ready for anyone who pops in.

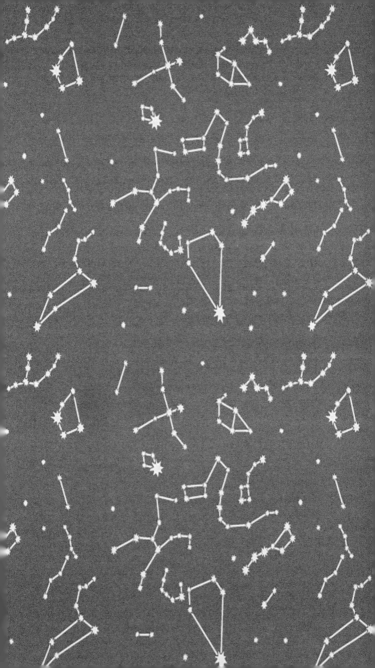

Your Star Sign Destinations

IDEAS FOR GEMINI:

- *ride a cable car in San Francisco*

- *visit a monkey sanctuary in Indonesia*

- *plan a cultural and culinary road trip through Spain*

Did you know that many cities and countries are ruled by a particular star sign? This is based on when a country was founded, although, depending on their history, sometimes places have more than one star sign attributed to them.

This can help you decide where to go on holiday and it can also explain why there are certain places where you feel at home straight away.

Gemini is associated with short trips, and you don't need to go far from home to enjoy yourself. If you live in a big city, you can be quite happy embracing a staycation and checking out all the local culture and sights.

Plonk a Gemini in a new town or city, and it won't take you long to find the most exciting areas off the beaten track. If there's music, activities, laughter and people, you're in your element. You love to check out the local flea markets and second-hand bookshops, or sit in a cafe in the middle of the main thoroughfare or market square and people-watch.

Road trips are ideal for Gemini too. You often prefer to explore different areas on holiday rather than stay in one place for too long.

If you are on a week-long holiday in a single destination, at the very least you must be there with your friends or meet interesting people. You do like to have fun on holiday, and colourful nightlife and plenty of lively activity, shenanigans, fun and games, suits your sign's mischievous nature.

If you're travelling alone, your best bet is to team up with a group of like-minded people on a study course or join up with a tour group exploring the sights and sounds of a new country together.

Wherever you are in the world, you won't want to sit in one place for too long. You love to walk and explore and be on the go. Even when you're tired, you'd still prefer to hop on a city tour bus so you can learn something new and see the sights all at the same time.

Countries ruled by Gemini include Wales, Belgium, Armenia

Cities ruled by Gemini include London in the UK; San Francisco in the USA; Melbourne in Australia; Bruges in Belgium; Nuremberg in Germany; Cardiff in Wales; Cordoba in Spain

Your Career and Vocation

When it comes to finding career fulfilment, it's imperative as a Gemini that you can diversify and try your hand at different roles and professions. In fact, it suits you to have more than one job at the same time, as it's a Gemini nightmare to be doing the same thing day in, day out.

Also, it's crucial when it comes to your working life that you enjoy what you're doing. If a job doesn't bring you fun and you find it annoying and dull, you won't last long. Similarly, you're not made for office jobs where you have to sit at your desk for hours on end pushing paper. At the very least, there must be good banter with your colleagues.

If you are in a traditional work role, see if you can wangle working from home a couple of days a week, to ring the changes. In work as well in life, you're at your best when you're on the move, not stuck in one place.

In fact, you'd probably prefer to be out and about running errands rather than holed up in an airless office. Working in a career that involves transport or travel where you visit different places, cities or countries can tick a lot of boxes to deliver Gemini satisfaction.

You are, however, made for any role where you're dealing with people regularly, whether you work in sales or you are on the phone handling enquiries. Your busy Gemini mind prefers to be in an environment that's fast-paced and lively with lots of customer contact. Having no one to talk to all day is rarely fun for sociable Gemini.

It's a similar story if you're in a job in, for example, a shop and the place is quiet all day long. It won't be long before you're creating your own stories and using your imagination to make time go faster. If you don't come into contact with other people or learn anything new, you quickly begin to feel unfulfilled.

The area where you excel and where many Gemini whizz-kids gather is the world of media. This is your domain, whether you work in television, radio, newspapers or magazines. The world of ideas, gossip, presenting and reporting is right up your alley because you're able to do what you do best – communicate, gather information, pass on what you know and entertain.

Any profession that's buzzing and lively will grab your attention, and because you don't have a long attention span, you love the constantly changing world of the media. Stories come and go; everyone's talking about a particular celebrity or idea for a short space of time, and then you're on to the next thing.

Your love of communication can take you into many different areas, whether you favour marketing, you love the world of spin, you want to teach and inspire other people or you adore learning and speaking languages. The spoken and written word are twin loves of the Gemini archetype. Finding a way to give expression to your thoughts, ideas and creativity is your ultimate vocation.

Also, if someone asks you to stand in front of a group of people and tell stories or share your knowledge or expertise, this skill usually comes naturally, and you often discover you love stepping into the role of presenter. Working with people on a one-to-one basis isn't your forte, however, and you tend to feel more comfortable within a group dynamic.

Not all Gemini individuals are extroverts who enjoy taking centre stage, but you do need an outlet in your career for your smart brain. You not only have a way with words, but your insatiable curiosity means you're a real ideas generator. In fact, the Gemini brain can be an information superhighway, which works at top speed to deliver interesting snippets.

You're rarely one of the most ambitious signs of the zodiac, however, nor especially practical. Instead, it's your boundless energy, your quick thinking, your love of life and people and the fact that you don't have time to stop for criticism that propel you to success.

You can slip into the instant results, social side of any career, instead of focusing on the long-term plan. This is not your forte, and you are someone who is easily sidetracked or distracted. You can fall down by leaving projects unfinished and not seeing ideas through to completion.

Work to your strengths, but at the same time, slow down and aim to create results over time. Either that or team up with other people who can help to turn your ideas into reality.

If you're seeking inspiration for a new job, take a look at the list below, which reveals the traditional careers that come under the Gemini archetype:

TRADITIONAL GEMINI CAREERS

writer
media representative
spin doctor
tennis player
tour guide

market trader

magician

TV broadcaster

radio presenter

telephone operator

sales/advertising executive

reporter

post office worker

journalist

teacher

linguist

voice actor

cycle courier

YouTube personality

graphologist

Your Money and Prosperity

> **KEY CONCEPTS:** buying and selling, two of everything, automatic money systems, gift of the blarney

The name of your ruling planet, Mercury, remains in use in modern-day language as the derivation of the words 'merchant' and 'merchandise', and it's also said to be the root of the word 'market'.

This makes sense because in mythology Mercury was the god of commerce and trade, involved in the exchange of goods, buying and selling. Money and prosperity is Gemini's stamping ground, and it's where you excel.

If you want to make money fast, use your gift of the gab down at the market and persuade people to buy what you're selling with your clever use of language and your social skills. You not only have a fast patter, but you know how to win people over with your quick wit. You are the zodiac's archetypal wheeler-dealer.

If you're a typical Gemini, you make a brilliant shopkeeper or trader. It's not surprising, therefore, that Mary Portas (28 May), one of the UK's top authorities on retail with the apt nickname, Mary Queen of Shops, is a Gemini.

The other reason why buying and selling is Gemini's domain is that you have a good eye for the latest gadgets or trends. You could do well setting up an internet shop and being the first to sell whatever's in fashion, and what consumers want or need to buy. Making a quick buck is ideal for your speedy Gemini nature.

When it comes to spending and saving money, this is where your mercurial nature kicks in. You are one of the zodiac's impulse buyers because you rarely stop to think for too long. If something looks like a bargain or is a must-have purchase, you leap in straight away. It might only be when you get back home that you wonder what on earth you were thinking.

As a Gemini, you love to buy two of everything. In your head, this saves you time and is an efficient way of shopping. Also, it means that when you spot the perfect item of clothing, it doesn't matter if one item gets damaged or lost, as you have the replacement immediately to hand.

If you're a typical Gemini, your busy mind doesn't always remember where you put things, and you do have a tendency to lose items easily. This is why you might think it's a good idea to splash out and buy the latest gadgets that can help you find your keys or phone.

Money tends to slip through your fingers if you're not careful. Also, you have an impulsive nature, and you often live for the moment rather than choose to save for a rainy day. It's a good idea for you to automate your money and set up systems that take care of the critical bills and savings, so you don't have to pay attention to your finances every month.

You do have to be careful that you don't exaggerate your wheeler-dealer tendencies to such an extent that you turn into a petty crook, whether it's intentional or not.

You can talk your way in or out of any situation, and it's easy for you to convince yourself and other people that you're doing nothing wrong by avoiding tax or filing the same invoice twice, for example. Use your gift of the blarney and your silver tongue to boost your prosperity in genuine ways rather than sliding into snake-oil salesman territory or ducking and diving.

Your Cosmic Gifts and Talents

The Now Age

If you're a typical Gemini, you live in the present day, rather than the past or the future. The here and now is where your interest is primarily focused. You respond instantly to life and live in the moment. Tim Berners-Lee (8 June) was a Gemini and the inventor of WWW, the World Wide Web.

The internet and modern technology in general play a significant role in keeping life immediate and relevant. Whether through blogging or keeping up to date with trends or the latest information, your sign of Gemini defines the Now Age.

Light Feet, Quick Hands

The classic Gemini has quick hands, and you might even be born ambidextrous. Use your hands, especially if you have a skill for craft-making, calligraphy or drawing. You might be a multi-instrumentalist with a gift for music or have a talent for sign language, semaphore or Morse code. Combine your quick hands with your light feet, and you can be an athlete, a gymnast, a tennis player. The Gemini archetype is nimble and agile; utilise your cosmic gifts to the best of your ability.

Language Expert

You are the linguist of the zodiac, the language connoisseur, and it's vital that you find a way to get your voice heard. You could pursue a linguistic profession, champion the power of language, be a voice actor or speak up for people who have no voice. In mythology, your ruler Mercury was linked to reading and writing, which were revered as magical and mystical arts. Today, the three Rs are a basic necessity in the western world, but that's not the case everywhere. Be an ambassador for language and keep the lines of communication wide open.

Second Names

You are the wordsmith of the zodiac, and you have a dual nature, so grab yourself a second name. This might come in the form of a double-barrelled surname, a pun on your real name or a nickname that sticks. Some Gemini individuals take this a stage further and create a stage name, develop an alter ego – or revert to a second name for duplicitous reasons. Whatever you choose, have fun with your name, experiment and, with your two names, stand out.

Student Of Life

As a Gemini, you have a search engine for a brain, and your insatiable curiosity and love of learning remains your whole life long. Your age doesn't matter; you are a certified student of life, always eager to discover, explore, pick up knowledge and tips, talk, share ideas, discuss and debate. Keep your mind lively by staying engaged with life, and use your astute brain to its optimum potential.

Mischief-Maker

You are the mischief-maker of the zodiac and enjoy yourself when you're out in the world having fun. Comedians such as ventriloquist Nina Conti (5 June) and impressionist Debra Stephenson (4 June) make the most of their Gemini funny and mimicking nature.

Also, only a Gemini could immortalise the role of Willy Wonka in *Charlie and the Chocolate*

Factory. The first actor to play Willy Wonka was Gene Wilder (11 June) and the second was Johnny Depp (9 June). Two Gemini actors, two films, one iconic mischief-making role.

Words and Numbers

Words are Gemini's weapon and you find writers, poets and top lyricists born under your sign, including legendary songwriters Bob Dylan (24 May) and Paul McCartney (18 June). However, your planet Mercury is not only associated with language and the written word but with arithmetic too.

If you have a gift for numbers, like mathematician John Forbes Nash (13 June), double Nobel Prize winner and the subject of the Hollywood movie, *A Beautiful Mind*, make the most of it. Be a whizz with words or numbers, or ideally both.

Films, Books, Music

· · · · ·

Films: The Toy Story franchise – Buzz Lightyear is voiced by Tim Allen (13 June) – or *Million Dollar Baby*, director Clint Eastwood (31 May)

Books: *The Carpetbaggers* by Harold Robbins (May 21), *Where The Wild Things Are* by Maurice Sendak (10 June) or Anne Frank's (12 June) diary

Music: You are THE rapper of the zodiac – Tupac Shakur (16 June), Lauryn Hill (26 May), Andre 3000 (27 May), Iggy Azalea (7 June), Kanye West (8 June), Azealia Banks (31 May), Ice Cube (15 June), Kendrick Lamar (17 June), The Notorious B.I.G. (21 May)

YOGA POSE:

Eagle: strengthens arms and legs, improves balance and focus

TAROT CARD:

The Magician

GIFTS TO BUY A GEMINI:

- silver bracelet
- magazine subscription
- set of pens
- manicure voucher
- membership to a talks venue
- electronic reader
- leather gloves
- video camera
- a pair of travel cases
- Star Gift – a timeshare apartment

Gemini Celebrities Born On Your Birthday

MAY

21 Harold Robbins, Fats Waller, Mr T., The Notorious B.I.G, Noel Fielding

22 Laurence Olivier, Charles Aznavour, Arthur Conan Doyle, Harvey Milk, George Best, Dale Winton, Denise Welch, Morrissey, Naomi Campbell, Katie Price, Novak Djokovic, Ginnifer Goodwin

Joan Collins, Drew Carey, Bob Mortimer, Eric Cantona, Ricky Gutierrez, Jewel, Jason Nash

 Queen Victoria, Bob Dylan, Priscilla Presley, Jim Broadbent, Kristin Scott Thomas, Dermot O'Leary

 Richard Dimbleby, Raymond Carver, Frank Oz, Ian McKellen, Alastair Campbell, Julian Clary, Octavia Spencer, Mike Myers, Cillian Murphy, Molly Sims, Lauryn Hill, Jonny Wilkinson, Anne Heche

 Peter Cushing, Isadora Duncan, Peggy Lee, Sally Ride, John Wayne, Miles Davis, Pam Grier, Stevie Nicks, Lenny Kravitz, Helena Bonham Carter, Scott Disick, Michael Portillo

 Vincent Price, Christopher Lee, Cilla Black, Paul Gascoigne, Joseph Fiennes,

Lisa Lopes, Denise van Outen, Jamie Oliver, Andre 3000, Paul Bettany

28 Ian Fleming, Gladys Knight, Faith Brown, Sondra Locke, Christa Miller, David Baddiel, Kylie Minogue, Brian Friedman, Mary Portas, Jonnie Peacock, Carey Mulligan

29 Bob Hope, John F. Kennedy, Danny Elfman, Annette Bening, Melissa Etheridge, Noel Gallagher, Mel B., Carol Kirkwood, Laverne Cox

30 Mel Blanc, Harry Enfield, Tom Morello, Duncan Jones, Marissa Mayer

31 Clint Eastwood, Lynda Bellingham, Dennis Rodman, Brooke Shields, Katie Hopkins, Colin Farrell, Ella Woodward, Reggie Banks, Azealia Banks

JUNE

 1 Marilyn Monroe, Morgan Freeman, Jonathan Pryce, Jason Donovan, Heidi Klum, Alanis Morissette, Sarah Wayne Callies, Tom Holland, Amy Schumer, Willow Shields

 2 Charlie Watts, Wentworth Miller, Zachary Quinto, Jewel Staite

 3 Josephine Baker, Tony Curtis, Curtis Mayfield, Rafael Nadal, Jodie Whittaker, Michelle Keegan, Anderson Cooper, Imogen Poots

 4 Bruce Dern, Geoffrey Palmer, Bradley Walsh, Debra Stephenson, Angelina Jolie, Russell Brand, Bar Refaeli, Noah Wyle

5 Kenny G., Mel Giedroyc, Mark Wahlberg, Nina Conti

6 Bjorn Borg, Paul Burrell, Paul Giamatti, Sandra Bernhard

7 Paul Gauguin, Dean Martin, Tom Jones, Liam Neeson, Prince, Damien Hirst, Anna Kournikova, Bear Grylls, Iggy Azalea

8 Tim Berners-Lee, Frank Lloyd Wright, Joan Rivers, Bonnie Tyler, Mick Hucknall, Shilpa Shetty, Kanye West, Julianna Margulies

9 Cole Porter, Charles Saatchi, Les Paul, Patricia Cornwell, Michael J. Fox, Johnny Depp, Natalie Portman, Matthew Bellamy

10 Prince Philip, Judy Garland, Maurice Sendak, Robert Maxwell, Elizabeth Hurley, Bill Burr

11 Gene Wilder, Diana Moran, Vince Lombardi, Joe Montana, Hugh Laurie, Jane Goldman, Shia LaBeouf, Claire Holt

12 George Bush, Anne Frank, Adriana Lima, Richard Ayoade

 13 Mary Whitehouse, Tim Allen, John Forbes Nash, Stellan Skarsgård, Kathy Burke, Kym Marsh, Ashley Olsen, Mary-Kate Olsen, Chris Evans, Kat Jennings

14 Donald Trump, Paul O'Grady, Boy George, Steffi Graf, Alan Carr, Yasmine Bleeth, Lucy Hale

15 Simon Callow, Jim Belushi, Johnny Hallyday, Helen Hunt, Courteney Cox, Ice Cube, Nadine Coyle, Neil Patrick Harris, Leah Remini

 16 Stan Laurel, Giacomo Agostini, Eddie Cibrian, Tupac Shakur

 17 M. C. Escher, Barry Manilow, Greg Kinnear, Venus Williams, Kendrick Lamar

18 Isabella Rossellini, Delia Smith, Paul McCartney, Blake Shelton

19 Lou Gehrig, Wallis Simpson, Salman Rushdie, Kathleen Turner, Paula Abdul, Aidan Turner, Zoe Saldana, Paul Dano, Jean Dujardin, Nick Drake, Boris Johnson

20 Errol Flynn, Brian Wilson, Lionel Richie, Nicole Kidman, Josh Lucas, John Goodman

21 Jane Russell, Ray Davies, Edward Snowden, Juliette Lewis, Chris Pratt, Lana Del Rey

Q&A Section

• • • • •

Q. What is the difference between a Sun sign and a Star sign?

A. They are the same thing. The Sun spends one month in each of the twelve star signs every year, so if you were born on 1 January, you are a Sun Capricorn. In astronomy, the Sun is termed a star rather than a planet, which is why the two names are interchangeable. The term 'zodiac sign', too, means the same as Sun sign and Star sign and is another way of describing which one of the twelve star signs you are, e.g. Sun Capricorn.

Q. What does it mean if I'm born on the cusp?

A. Being born on the cusp means that you were born on a day when the Sun moves from one of the twelve zodiac signs into the next. However, the Sun doesn't change signs at the same time each year. Sometimes it can be a day earlier or a day later. In the celebrity birthday section of the book, names in brackets mean that this person's birthday falls into this category.

If you know your complete birth data, including the date, time and place you were born, you can find out definitively what Sun sign you are. You do this by either checking an ephemeris (a planetary table) or asking an astrologer. For example, if a baby were born on 20 January 2018, it would be Sun Capricorn if born before 03:09 GMT or Sun Aquarius if born after 03:09 GMT. A year earlier, the Sun left Capricorn a day earlier and entered Aquarius on 19 January 2017, at 21:24 GMT. Each year the time changes are slightly different.

Q. Has my sign of the zodiac changed since I was born?

A. Every now and again, the media talks about a new sign of the zodiac called Ophiuchus and about there now being thirteen signs. This means that you're unlikely to be the same Sun sign as you always thought you were.

This method is based on fixing the Sun's movement to the star constellations in the sky, and is called 'sidereal' astrology. It's used traditionally in India and other Asian countries.

The star constellations are merely namesakes for the twelve zodiac signs. In western astrology, the zodiac is divided into twelve equal parts that are in sync with the seasons. This method is called 'tropical' astrology. The star constellations and the zodiac signs aren't the same.

Astrology is based on a beautiful pattern of symmetry (see Additional Information) and it wouldn't be the same if a thirteenth sign were introduced into the pattern. So never fear, no one is going to have to say their star sign is Ophiuchus, a name nobody even knows how to pronounce!

Q. Is astrology still relevant to me if I was born in the southern hemisphere?

A. Yes, astrology is unquestionably relevant to you. Astrology's origins, however, were founded in the northern hemisphere, which is why the Spring Equinox coincides with the Sun's move into Aries, the first sign of the zodiac. In the southern hemisphere, the seasons are reversed. Babylonian, Egyptian and Greek and Roman astrology are the forebears of modern-day astrology, and all of these civilisations were located in the northern hemisphere.

● ● ● ● ●

Q. Should I read my Sun sign, Moon sign and Ascendant sign?

A. If you know your horoscope or you have drawn up an astrology wheel for the time of your birth, you will be aware that you are more than your Sun sign. The Sun is the most important star in the sky, however, because the other planets revolve around it, and your horoscope in the media is based on Sun signs. The Sun represents your essence, who you are striving to become throughout your lifetime.

The Sun, Moon and Ascendant together give you a broader impression of yourself as all three reveal further elements about your personality. If you know your Moon and Ascendant signs, you can read all three books to gain further insight into who you are. It's also a good idea to read the Sun sign book that relates to your partner, parents, children, best friends, even your boss for a better understanding of their characters too.

Q. Is astrology a mix of fate and free will?

A. Yes. Astrology is not causal, i.e. the planets don't cause things to happen in your life; instead, the two are interconnected, hence the saying 'As above, so below'. The symbolism of the planets' movements mirrors what's happening on earth and in your personal experience of life.

You can choose to sit back and let your life unfold, or you can decide the best course of action available to you. In this way, you are combining your fate and free will, and this is one of astrology's major purposes in life. A knowledge of astrology can help you live more authentically, and it offers you a fresh perspective on how best to make progress in your life.

Q. What does it mean if I don't identify with my Sun sign? Is there a reason for this?

A. The majority of people identify with their Sun sign, and it is thought that one route to fulfilment is to grow into your Sun sign. You do get the odd exception, however.

For example, a Pisces man was adamant that he wasn't at all romantic, mystical, creative or caring, all typical Pisces archetypes. It turned out he'd spent the whole of his adult life working in the oil industry and lived primarily on the sea. Neptune is one of Pisces' ruling planets and god of the sea and Pisces rules all liquids, including oil. There's the Pisces connection.

Q. What's the difference between astrology and astronomy?

A. Astrology means 'language of the stars', whereas astronomy means 'mapping of the stars'. Traditionally, they were considered one discipline, one form of study and they coexisted together for many hundreds of years. Since the dawn of the Scientific Age, however, they have split apart.

Astronomy is the scientific strand, calculating and logging the movement of the planets, whereas astrology is the interpretation of the movement of the stars. Astrology works on a symbolic and intuitive level to offer guidance and insight. It reunites you with a universal truth, a knowingness that can sometimes get lost in place of an objective, scientific truth. Both are of value.

Q. What is a cosmic marriage in astrology?

A. One of the classic indicators of a relationship that's a match made in heaven is the union of the Sun and Moon. When they fall close to each other in the same sign in the birth charts of you and your partner, this is called a cosmic marriage. In astrology, the Sun and Moon are the king and queen of the heavens; the Sun is a masculine energy, and the Moon a feminine energy. They represent the eternal cycle of day and night, yin and yang.

Q. What does the Saturn Return mean?

A. In traditional astrology, Saturn was the furthest planet from the Sun, representing boundaries and the end of the universe. Saturn is linked to karma and time, and represents authority, structure and responsibility. It takes Saturn twenty-nine to thirty years to make a complete cycle of the zodiac and return to the place where it was when you were born.

This is what people mean when they talk about their Saturn Return; it's the astrological coming of age. Turning thirty can be a soul-searching time, when you examine how far you've come in life and whether you're on the right track. It's a watershed moment, a reality check and a defining stage of adulthood. The decisions you make during your Saturn Return are crucial, whether they represent endings or new commitments. Either way, it's the start of an important stage in your life path.

Additional Information

● ● ● ● ●

The Symmetry of Astrology

There is a beautiful symmetry to the zodiac (see horoscope wheel). There are twelve zodiac signs, which can be divided into two sets of 'introvert' and 'extrovert' signs, four elements (fire, earth, air, water), three modes (cardinal, fixed, mutable) and six pairs of opposite signs.

One of the values of astrology is in bringing opposites together, showing how they complement each other and work together and, in so doing, restore unity. The horoscope wheel represents the cyclical nature of life.

Aries (*March 21–April 19*)
Taurus (*April 20–May 20*)
Gemini (*May 21–June 20*)
Cancer (*June 21–July 22*)
Leo (*July 23–August 22*)
Virgo (*August 23–September 22*)
Libra (*September 23–October 23*)
Scorpio (*October 24–November 22*)
Sagittarius (*November 23–December 21*)
Capricorn (*December 22–January 20*)
Aquarius (*January 21–February 18*)
Pisces (*February 19–March 20*)

ELEMENTS

There are four elements in astrology and three signs allocated to each. The elements are:

fire – Aries, Leo, Sagittarius
earth – Taurus, Virgo, Capricorn
air – Gemini, Libra, Aquarius
water – Cancer, Scorpio, Pisces

What each element represents:

Fire – fire blazes bright and fire types are inspirational, motivational, adventurous and love creativity and play

Earth – earth is grounding and solid, and earth rules money, security, practicality, the physical body and slow living

Air – air is intangible and vast and air rules thinking, ideas, social interaction, debate and questioning

Water – water is deep and healing and water rules feelings, intuition, quietness, relating, giving and sharing

MODES

There are three modes in astrology and four star signs allocated to each. The modes are:

cardinal – Aries, Cancer, Libra, Capricorn
fixed – Taurus, Leo, Scorpio, Aquarius
mutable – Gemini, Virgo, Sagittarius, Pisces

What each mode represents:

Cardinal – The first group represents the leaders of the zodiac, and these signs love to initiate and take action. Some say they're controlling.

Fixed – The middle group holds fast and stands the middle ground and acts as a stable, reliable companion. Some say they're stubborn.

Mutable – The last group is more willing to go with the flow and let life drift. They're more flexible and adaptable and often dual-natured. Some say they're all over the place.

INTROVERT AND EXTROVERT SIGNS/ OPPOSITE SIGNS

The introvert signs are the earth and water signs and the extrovert signs are the fire and air signs. Both sets oppose each other across the zodiac.

The 'introvert' earth and water oppositions are:

- Taurus – • Scorpio
- Cancer – • Capricorn
- Virgo – • Pisces

The 'extrovert' air and fire oppositions are:

- Aries – • Libra
- Gemini – • Sagittarius
- Leo – • Aquarius

THE HOUSES

The houses of the astrology wheel are an additional component to Sun sign horoscopes. The symmetry that is inherent within astrology remains, as the wheel is divided into twelve equal sections, called 'houses'. Each of the twelve houses is governed by one of the twelve zodiac signs.

There is an overlap in meaning as you move round the houses. Once you know the symbolism of all the star signs, it can be fleshed out further by learning about the areas of life represented by the twelve houses.

The houses provide more specific information if you choose to have a detailed birth chart reading.

This is based not only on your day of birth, which reveals your star sign, but also your time and place of birth. Here's the complete list of the meanings of the twelve houses and the zodiac sign they are ruled by:

1 – **Aries:** self, physical body, personal goals

2 – **Taurus:** money, possessions, values

3 – **Gemini:** communication, education, siblings, local neighbourhood

4 – **Cancer:** home, family, roots, the past, ancestry

5 – **Leo:** creativity, romance, entertainment, children, luck

6 – **Virgo:** work, routine, health, service

7 – **Libra:** relationships, the 'other', enemies, contracts

8 – **Scorpio:** joint finances, other people's resources, all things hidden and taboo

9 – **Sagittarius:** travel, study, philosophy, legal affairs, publishing, religion

10 – **Capricorn:** career, vocation, status, reputation

11 – **Aquarius:** friends, groups, networks, social responsibilities

12 – **Pisces:** retreat, sacrifice, spirituality

A GUIDE TO LOVE MATCHES

The star signs relate to each other in different ways depending on their essential nature. It can also be helpful to know the pattern they create across the zodiac. Here's a quick guide that relates to the chapter on Love Matches:

Two Peas In A Pod – the same star sign

Opposites Attract – star signs opposite each other

Soulmates – five or seven signs apart, and a traditional 'soulmate' connection

In Your Element – four signs apart, which means you share the same element

Squaring Up To Each Other – three signs apart, which means you share the same mode

Sexy Sextiles – two signs apart, which means you're both 'introverts' or 'extroverts'

Next Door Neighbours – one sign apart, different in nature but often share close connections